Worl

MW00950657

for

Finding Your Nxt:

A practice guide on When You're Ready for the Life You Really Want

Aviana Print

Table of content

Table of content 3

How to Use This Workbook 4

Introduction 7

Summary 9

The Nxt Journey 13

    Key Lessons: 13

    Reflection Prompts: 14

What's Your Nxt? 20

    Key Lessons: 20

    Reflection Prompts: 21

The Nxt Steps 27

    Key Lessons: 27

    Reflection Prompts: 28

The Nxt Life 34

    Key Lessons: 34

The Nxt You 42

    Key Lessons: 42

    Reflection Prompts: 43

The Nxt Now 49

    Key Lessons 49

    Self-Assessment 56

Checklist 64

conclusion 66

How to Use This Workbook

Welcome to the companion workbook for [Title of the Original Book]. This workbook has been designed to help you dive deeper into the content of the original book, gain a better understanding of its key concepts, and apply them to your life. Whether you've already read the book or you're just starting, this workbook is a valuable resource to enhance your learning experience.

Workbook Overview

Summary of the Original Book: Begin your journey by revisiting the core ideas and messages of the original book. This section provides a concise summary, allowing you to refresh your memory and establish a solid foundation for the exercises and reflections that follow.

Chapter Key Lessons: As you progress through the workbook, you'll find sections dedicated to each chapter of the original book. In these sections, we've distilled the key lessons and insights from each chapter. Pay close attention to these summaries, as they serve as a roadmap for your self-improvement journey.

Self-Reflection Questions: After reviewing the chapter's key lessons, take the time to reflect on your own experiences and thoughts. We've provided thought-provoking self-reflection questions that encourage you to apply the book's concepts to your life. Use these questions to explore your personal insights, beliefs, and actions.

Self-Evaluation Questions: Towards the end of this workbook, you'll encounter a dedicated section for self-evaluation. Here, you can assess your progress and growth in light of the book's teachings. These questions are designed to help you measure your development and identify areas where further exploration or improvement may be necessary.

Checklist: To keep yourself organized and accountable, we've included a checklist. Use it to track your completion of each chapter's exercises and self-reflection questions. This checklist will help you stay on course and ensure you don't miss any critical steps in your self-improvement journey.

Getting the Most Out of This Workbook

To maximize the benefits of this workbook, consider the following tips:

Read the Original Book: If you haven't already, we recommend reading or revisiting the original book before using this workbook. This will provide you with a comprehensive understanding of the author's ideas.

Set Aside Dedicated Time: Allocate regular, uninterrupted time to work through this workbook. Reflecting on your thoughts and experiences can be a deeply rewarding process, but it requires focus and commitment.

Be Honest with Yourself: When answering self-reflection questions and completing self-evaluations, be honest and open with yourself. Growth often begins with self-awareness.

Connect with Others: Consider discussing your insights and reflections with friends, a book club, or an online community. Sharing your thoughts can lead to richer discussions and new perspectives.

Remember that this workbook is a tool for personal growth and exploration. It's here to guide you, challenge you, and ultimately help you apply the valuable lessons from the original book to your life. We encourage you to engage with it thoughtfully and consistently, and we wish you a transformative journey ahead.

Introduction

Life is a journey filled with unforeseen twists and turns. At times, we may feel as if we are aimlessly roaming, looking for a route that resonates with our actual selves. We crave for guidance, inspiration, and skills to help us discover the life we truly desire during these times of uncertainty. "Finding Your Next: When You're Ready for the Life You Really Want" is a compelling book that provides insightful insights about handling life's changes.

As you begin on this self-discovery adventure with "Finding Your Next," you'll immediately understand that the book is more than simply a guide; it's a road map to change. This book has touched the lives of countless people, sparking the flame of change inside them, thanks to the knowledge of its author, a seasoned expert in personal development.

However, we recognize that the road to self-discovery is extremely individualized, and there is no one-size-fits-all solution. This is where the unofficial workbook comes in. Our workbook, designed to supplement the insights offered in "Finding Your Next," gives you a hands-on, interactive experience that allows you to delve even further into the process of self-exploration and growth.

In these pages, you'll discover activities, prompts, and thoughts to help you pause, think, and take action toward the life you've always wanted. We believe that true change does not happen immediately, and that it frequently needs persistent work and contemplation. This workbook will be there for you every step of the journey.

Whether you're just starting out on your road of self-discovery or have been on it for a while, this workbook is a reliable companion. It is intended to meet you where you are, providing a safe area for self-reflection, goal setting, and personal development. It is not about hurrying through the process, but rather about relishing each moment and allowing yourself to mature at your own speed.

The unauthorized "Finding Your Next" workbook is not associated with the author or publisher. Instead, it's a labor of love made by people who have personally experienced the book's transformational effect. We feel so strongly in the idea of "Finding Your Next" that we wanted to provide this resource to assist you in delving further into your own journey.

So, as you go on this journey, keep in mind that you are not alone. With the knowledge in "Finding Your Next" as your guide and the activities in this workbook as your companions, you'll be able to realize your true potential and the life you truly desire. Accept the trip, have faith in the process, and let us go on this metamorphosis together.

Summary

Chapter 1: The Nxt Journey

In this chapter, Carrillo begins by defining the Nxt as "the next big thing in your life, the thing that will bring you more joy, satisfaction, and fulfillment." She then shares her own story of how she went from being a successful CEO to a "ranch girl" who births baby goats in her lap. She explains how finding her Nxt allowed her to live a more authentic and fulfilling life.

Carrillo then talks about the importance of finding your Nxt. She says that it's not something that happens to you, it's something that you create. She encourages you to think about what you really want out of life and to start taking steps towards making it happen.

Chapter 2: What's Your Nxt?

In this chapter, Carrillo helps you identify your own Nxt by asking you a series of questions about your values, passions, and strengths. She also provides exercises to help you clarify your vision for your Nxt and to overcome any fears or obstacles that may be holding you back.

Some of the questions Carrillo asks include:

What are your core values?

What are you passionate about?

What are you good at?

What are you excited about?

What are you afraid of?

What are the obstacles in your way?

Carrillo also provides exercises such as vision boards and journaling to help you clarify your vision for your Nxt and to overcome any fears or obstacles that may be holding you back.

Chapter 3: The Nxt Steps

In this chapter, Carrillo provides practical advice on how to make your Nxt happen. She covers topics such as setting goals, creating a plan, and overcoming challenges. She also shares stories of people who have successfully achieved their Nxts.

Some of the advice Carrillo gives includes:

Set specific, measurable, achievable, relevant, and time-bound goals.

Create a plan that outlines the steps you need to take to achieve your goals.

Be prepared to overcome challenges.

Don't be afraid to ask for help.

Celebrate your successes along the way.

Chapter 4: The Nxt Life

In this chapter, Carrillo talks about what it's like to live your Nxt life. She shares her insights on how to stay motivated, overcome challenges, and enjoy the journey. She also provides advice on how to create a legacy that will last.

Some of the insights Carrillo shares include:

The Nxt life is not always easy, but it's always worth it.

You need to be willing to step outside of your comfort zone.

You need to be persistent and never give up on your dreams.

You need to surround yourself with positive people who support you.

You need to leave a legacy behind that makes a difference in the world.

Chapter 5: The Nxt You

In this chapter, Carrillo challenges you to become the Nxt version of yourself. She encourages you to step outside of your comfort zone, take risks, and live your life to the fullest. She also provides advice on how to create a life that is truly meaningful to you.

Some of the challenges Carrillo encourages you to take include:

Try something new every day.

Say yes to opportunities that scare you.

Take a risk on yourself.

Live in the present moment.

Be grateful for what you have.

Chapter 6: The Nxt Now

In this chapter, Carrillo reminds you that you don't have to wait for the Nxt to start living your best life. She encourages you to start taking steps towards your Nxt today, even if it's just one small step at a time.

Carrillo says that the Nxt is not about waiting for the perfect moment, it's about taking action and creating your own destiny. She encourages you to start living your Nxt life today, and to never give up on your dreams.

The Nxt Journey

Key Lessons:

1. Nxt is defined as the next major and meaningful phase in your life that can provide you joy and fulfillment.

2. Personal Transformation: Carrillo's personal transformation from CEO to ranch girl demonstrates how drastic adjustments may lead to a more honest and fulfilled existence.

3. Nxt is developed actively, rather than passively, as a result of your activities and decisions.

4. Self-Reflection: Discovering your Nxt necessitates reflection and consideration of your genuine objectives and aspirations.

5. Authenticity: When you align with your Nxt, you may live a more authentic life.

6. Carrillo underlines the necessity of taking action toward your Nxt.

7. Living Authentically: The key to a more fulfilling existence is authenticity.

Reflection Prompts:

1. Have you ever had a life-changing encounter that caused you to reassess your path?

_____

_____

_____

_____

_____

_____

_____

_____

_____

_____

_____

_____

_____

_____

2. Consider a period when you actively pursued something that provided you with joy and fulfillment. What was it, and what did you discover?

_____

_____

_____

_____

_____

_____

_____

_____

_____

_____

_____

_____

_____

_____

_____

_____

3. How do you describe your Nxt now, and what measures have you taken to get there?

_____

_____

_____

_____

_____

_____

_____

_____

_____

_____

_____

_____

_____

_____

_____

_____

_____

_____

4. What components of your life feel genuine to you, and what don't?

_____

_____

_____

_____

_____

_____

_____

_____

_____

_____

_____

_____

_____

_____

_____

_____

_____

5. What is one step you can do now to get started on your Nxt?

_____

_____

_____

_____

_____

_____

_____

_____

_____

_____

_____

_____

_____

_____

_____

_____

_____

_____

_____

6. Share a personal story on how authenticity influenced your happiness and fulfillment.

_____

_____

_____

_____

_____

_____

_____

_____

_____

_____

_____

_____

_____

_____

_____

7. What do you think the connection is between honesty and fulfillment?

_____

_____

_____

_____

_____

_____

_____

_____

_____

_____

_____

_____

_____

_____

What's Your Nxt?

Key Lessons:

1, Introspection and Self-Awareness: Identifying your Nxt requires introspection and a grasp of your values, interests, and strengths.

2. Exercises like vision boards and writing can help you define your vision for your Nxt.

3. Overcoming difficulties: Recognizing and tackling worries and difficulties is critical in moving forward with your Nxt.

4. Individuality: Each person's Nxt is unique, and no universal formula exists.

5. Continuous Self-Discovery: Nxt is an ever-changing notion that evolves as you develop and learn.

6. Personal Development: Facing concerns and taking chances are crucial for personal growth.

7. Continual Change: Pursuing your Nxt necessitates ongoing development and change.

Reflection Prompts:

1. Consider your basic principles and how they impact your life choices.

_____

_____

_____

_____

_____

_____

_____

_____

_____

_____

_____

_____

_____

_____

_____

2. What creative exercises, such as vision boards or writing, have you done to define your objectives and aspirations?

_____

_____

_____

_____

_____

_____

_____

_____

_____

_____

_____

_____

_____

_____

3. Share a worry or impediment that has stymied your progress toward your Nxt. How do you intend to deal with it?

_____

_____

_____

_____

_____

_____

_____

_____

_____

_____

_____

_____

_____

4. In what ways do you embrace your individuality while you pursue your Nxt?

_____

_____

_____

_____

_____

_____

_____

_____

_____

_____

_____

_____

_____

_____

_____

5. How has your perception of your Nxt changed over time? What experiences or circumstances affected this evolution?

_____

_____

_____

_____

_____

_____

_____

_____

_____

_____

_____

_____

_____

_____

6. Describe a time when you took a risk that helped you grow as a person. What was the end result?

_____

_____

_____

_____

_____

_____

_____

_____

_____

_____

_____

_____

_____

_____

_____

_____

7. How do you envision your Nxt changing as you grow and change?

_____

_____

_____

_____

_____

_____

_____

_____

_____

_____

_____

_____

_____

The Nxt Steps

Key Lessons:

Setting clear, measurable, attainable, relevant, and time-bound (SMART) objectives is critical.

Strategic Planning: It is critical to have a well-defined strategy with concrete tasks in order to achieve your Nxt.

Challenges as opportunities: Obstacles are a necessary part of the trip and present opportunities for progress.

Seeking Help: Asking for assistance and surrounding yourself with a supportive network will hasten your success.

Milestone Recognition and Celebration: Recognizing and appreciating victories along the road keeps you motivated.

Learning from Others: Other people's success stories might give useful insights and motivation.

Consistent work and growth are essential for attaining your Nxt.

Reflection Prompts:

1. Can you think of a particular Nxt objective that you can transform into a smart goal?

_____

_____

_____

_____

_____

_____

_____

_____

_____

_____

_____

_____

_____

_____

2. How do you usually devise a strategy to attain your objectives? Is there anything you might do to better your planning process?

_____

_____

_____

_____

_____

_____

_____

_____

_____

_____

_____

_____

_____

_____

_____

3. Consider a difficulty you've encountered while pursuing your Nxt. What did you learn as a result of conquering it?

_____

_____

_____

_____

_____

_____

_____

_____

_____

_____

_____

_____

_____

4. that are the individuals in your life that are encouraging you on your Nxt journey? What role do they play in your advancement?

_____

_____

_____

_____

_____

_____

_____

_____

_____

_____

_____

_____

_____

_____

_____

_____

5. Share a recent accomplishment or milestone in your Nxt journey. How did you mark the occasion?

_____

_____

_____

_____

_____

_____

_____

_____

_____

_____

_____

_____

_____

_____

_____

_____

6. Consider someone you respect who has reached their Nxt. What can you take out from their experiences?

_____

_____

_____

_____

_____

_____

_____

_____

_____

_____

_____

_____

_____

_____

7. How do you keep your attempts to get closer to your Nxt consistent?

_____

_____

_____

_____

_____

_____

_____

_____

_____

_____

_____

_____

_____

_____

_____

_____

_____

The Nxt Life

Key Lessons:

1. Intrinsic Worth: The Nxt life may be difficult, but it is intrinsically valuable and worth the effort.

2. Getting Out of Your Comfort Zone: Getting out of your comfort zone is frequently necessary for growth.

3. Persistence: It is critical to maintain resolve and not give up on your ambitions in order to live your Nxt life.

4. Positive Surroundings: Surrounding oneself with positive, supportive people may substantially improve your path.

5. Leaving a Legacy: Making a lasting influence and making a difference in the world is an important aspect of Nxt life.

6. Continuous Evolution: The Nxt life is a never-ending journey of self-discovery and progress.

7. Accepting Difficulties and difficulties: Difficulties and difficulties are chances for personal growth.

Reflection Prompts:

1. Share a personal example in which you overcame obstacles to achieve a meaningful objective. What drove you to persevere?

_____

_____

_____

_____

_____

_____

_____

_____

_____

_____

_____

_____

_____

_____

_____

_____

2. Consider a time when you pushed yourself beyond your comfort zone.

_____

_____

_____

_____

_____

_____

_____

_____

_____

_____

_____

_____

_____

_____

_____

_____

3. How did this experience help you grow as a person?

_____

_____

_____

_____

_____

_____

_____

_____

_____

_____

_____

_____

_____

_____

_____

4. Describe a case in which persistence and dedication resulted in the accomplishment of an important goal.

_____

_____

_____

_____

_____

_____

_____

_____

_____

_____

_____

_____

_____

_____

_____

_____

5. Who are the individuals in your life who are positive and helpful, and how have they influenced your Nxt journey?

_____

_____

_____

_____

_____

_____

_____

_____

_____

_____

_____

_____

_____

_____

_____

_____

_____

6. What type of legacy do you hope to leave? How does this relate to your Nxt?

_____

_____

_____

_____

_____

_____

_____

_____

_____

_____

_____

_____

_____

_____

_____

7. How do you see your Nxt life changing over time, taking into account both problems and opportunities?

_____

_____

_____

_____

_____

_____

_____

_____

_____

_____

_____

_____

_____

_____

_____

_____

8. Can you think of a recent difficulty that contributed to your personal development and growth?

_____

_____

_____

_____

_____

_____

_____

_____

_____

_____

_____

_____

_____

_____

_____

_____

The Nxt You

Key Lessons:

1. Embrace Change: To become the Nxt version of yourself, you must venture outside of your comfort zone and embrace change.

2. Taking prudent risks and saying yes to chances can lead to considerable personal development.

3. Present-Mindedness: Living in the moment promotes a more satisfying life.

4. Gratitude: Being grateful for what you have improves your general well-being and contentment.

5. Continuous Improvement: Becoming the Nxt You is a never-ending process of self-improvement.

6. Conquering Fears: Overcoming fears and doubts is an important aspect of human development and self-discovery.

7. Engaging in new experiences and difficulties on a daily-basis leads to personal progress.

Reflection Prompts:

1. Consider a huge life change. What effect did it have on your own growth and development?

_____

_____

_____

_____

_____

_____

_____

_____

_____

_____

_____

_____

_____

_____

2. Give an example of a calculated risk that resulted in positive personal progress. What did the experience teach you?

_____

_____

_____

_____

_____

_____

_____

_____

_____

_____

_____

_____

_____

_____

_____

_____

3. Consider how you live in the present moment in your daily existence. What advantages have you noticed?

_____

_____

_____

_____

_____

_____

_____

_____

_____

_____

_____

_____

_____

_____

4. What do you actually appreciate in your life, and how does this affect your overall happiness?

_____

_____

_____

_____

_____

_____

_____

_____

_____

_____

_____

_____

_____

_____

_____

_____

5. How do you see yourself developing and improving in order to become the Nxt version of yourself?

_____

_____

_____

_____

_____

_____

_____

_____

_____

_____

_____

_____

_____

_____

_____

_____

6. Describe an opportunity that first worried you but eventually aided your personal growth.

_____

_____

_____

_____

_____

_____

_____

_____

_____

_____

_____

_____

_____

_____

_____

_____

_____

7. How can you incorporate fresh experiences and daily challenges
into your life to promote continual self-improvement?

_____

_____

_____

_____

_____

_____

_____

_____

_____

_____

_____

_____

_____

_____

_____

_____

_____

The Nxt Now

Key Lessons:

1. Immediate Action: You don't have to wait for the ideal time to begin chasing your Nxt; taking action immediately is critical.

2. Personal Responsibility: Creating your own future through your activities is central to Nxt.

3. tiny moves Count: Taking tiny moves on a regular basis is more beneficial than waiting for big possibilities.

4. Procrastination Slows Progress: Procrastination slows down your progress toward your Nxt.

5. Ongoing Journey: Your Nxt journey is ongoing, and you must adjust to new conditions.

6. Persistence: A strong confidence in your dreams, as well as consistent work, are essential for success.

7. Nxt Begins Now: Your Nxt life may begin today, no matter where you are on your journey.

Reflection Prompts:

1. What one tiny, practical step can you take today to get closer to your Nxt?

_____

_____

_____

_____

_____

_____

_____

_____

_____

_____

_____

_____

_____

_____

_____

_____

2. Consider your part in shaping your own future. How do your activities influence your route to your Nxt?

_____

_____

_____

_____

_____

_____

_____

_____

_____

_____

_____

_____

_____

_____

_____

_____

3. Tell us about a time when taking regular tiny measures resulted in great success in your life.

_____

_____

_____

_____

_____

_____

_____

_____

_____

_____

_____

_____

_____

_____

_____

4. How can you battle procrastination and keep it from impeding your progress toward your Nxt?

_____

_____

_____

_____

_____

5. Consider how you respond to changes in your Nxt journey. What methods do you employ?

_____

_____

_____

_____

_____

_____

_____

_____

6. Consider a period when your perseverance and unshakeable confidence in your ambitions were critical to your achievement.

_____

_____

_____

_____

_____

_____

_____

_____

_____

_____

_____

_____

_____

_____

_____

_____

7. How can you remind yourself that your Nxt life starts today, regardless of your existing situation?

_____

_____

_____

_____

_____

_____

_____

_____

_____

_____

_____

_____

_____

_____

_____

_____

_____

Self-Assessment

1. Have you given serious thought to what you actually want out of life, taking into account your basic values, interests, strengths, anxieties, and obstacles?

_____

_____

_____

_____

_____

_____

_____

_____

_____

_____

_____

_____

_____

_____

_____

_____

_____

2. Authenticity Check: Consider which elements of your life correspond with your genuine self and which feel inauthentic. What measures can you take to increase the level of authenticity in your life?

_____

_____

_____

_____

_____

_____

_____

_____

_____

_____

_____

_____

_____

_____

_____

3. Taking Action: Are you actively pursuing your Nxt, or are you waiting for the "perfect" moment?

_____

_____

_____

_____

_____

_____

_____

_____

_____

_____

_____

_____

_____

_____

_____

_____

_____

4, Have you established SMART (specific, measurable, attainable, relevant, and time-bound) goals for your Nxt?

_____

_____

_____

_____

_____

_____

_____

_____

_____

_____

_____

_____

_____

_____

_____

_____

5. Think about the individuals in your life. Are there people who are encouraging and supportive of your Nxt journey? How can you strengthen these bonds?

_____

_____

_____

_____

_____

_____

_____

_____

_____

_____

_____

_____

_____

_____

_____

_____

6. What type of legacy do you want to leave, and how does it relate to your Nxt?

_____

_____

_____

_____

_____

_____

_____

_____

_____

_____

_____

_____

_____

_____

_____

_____

_____

7. How do you see hurdles and roadblocks in your journey?

_____

_____

_____

_____

_____

_____

_____

_____

_____

_____

_____

_____

_____

_____

_____

_____

_____

8. Do you perceive them as possibilities for personal growth and development?

_____

_____

_____

_____

Checklist

Define your own concept of "Nxt" in your life.

[ ] Reflect on any significant personal transformations or radical changes you've experienced.[ ] [ ] Evaluate whether you actively create your own path to your Nxt or wait for opportunities.

[ ] Engage in deep self-reflection to identify your core values, passions, strengths, fears, and obstacles.

[ ] Align your life choices with authenticity and consider areas where you may not be true to yourself.

[ ] Begin taking concrete actions toward your Nxt, no matter how small they may seem.

[ ] Set SMART goals (specific, measurable, achievable, relevant, and time-bound) related to your Nxt.

[ ] Develop a clear plan outlining the steps needed to achieve your Nxt.

[ ] View challenges and obstacles as opportunities for growth and learning.

[ ] Seek support from positive and supportive individuals who can enhance your Nxt journey.

[ ] Celebrate your successes and milestones along the way to stay motivated.

[ ] Consider the legacy you want to leave behind and how it aligns with your Nxt.

[ ] Embrace change and step out of your comfort zone to become the next version of yourself.

[ ] Take calculated risks and say "yes" to opportunities for personal growth.

[ ] Cultivate mindfulness and gratitude in your daily life.

[ ] Recognize that your journey to your Nxt is a continuous process of self-improvement and evolution.

[ ] Confront and conquer your fears and uncertainties.

[ ] Embrace daily challenges and new experiences as avenues for personal development.

[ ] Understand that you don't need to wait for the "perfect" moment to start pursuing your Nxt.

[ ] Recognize your role in creating your own destiny through your actions.

[ ] Consistently take small steps toward your Nxt, avoiding procrastination.

[ ] Adapt to changing circumstances and continue to evolve in your Nxt journey.

[ ] Maintain unwavering belief in your dreams and demonstrate persistence.

[ ] Acknowledge that your Nxt life can begin today, regardless of your current situation or progress.

conclusion

We've taken a transforming trip through the pages of this book, delving into the notion of "Nxt" - the next great thing in our lives that promises joy, happiness, and fulfillment. We've dug into the art of defining, pursuing, and accepting our particular routes to a more genuine and meaningful living thanks to the author's knowledge and insights.

The notion of Nxt as given here is more than just a place to go; it is a dynamic force that encourages us to question the existing quo, seek self-discovery, and actively change our futures. As we come to the end of our trip, it is critical that we reflect on the main lessons that will enable us to continue our pursuit of Nxt in our life.

First and foremost, we've discovered that Nxt is a personal and one-of-a-kind enterprise. It is not a predetermined destiny that awaits us, but rather a blank canvas on which we may paint our dreams, ideals, and passions. It inspires us to think thoroughly about what genuinely matters to us and what we want our lives to represent.

Most importantly, we've understood that Nxt necessitates action. It is not a passive game of waiting, but rather an active quest. We've noticed that taking continuous actions towards our Nxt is the most effective approach to actualize our wishes, whether it's setting SMART goals, making plans, or accepting change.

This experience has also highlighted the need of sincerity. Aligning our lives with our fundamental beliefs and interests, as well as venturing beyond of our comfort zones when required, promotes a sense of fulfillment that cannot be found in compliance or compromise. Embracing and embodying our genuine selves becomes the driving force behind the Nxt.

We've also learned the importance of resilience and tenacity throughout the book. Carrillo's journey from successful CEO to "ranch girl" indicates that the route to Nxt is frequently fraught with difficulties. But it is precisely these difficulties that make the journey worthwhile. We've observed that confronting challenges straight on, surrounding ourselves with a supporting network, and celebrating our victories along the road keep us motivated and on track.

Legacy has also emerged as a major subject. Making a difference in the world and leaving a lasting impression is an essential aspect of the Nxt way of life. We've been urged to think about the legacy we want to leave behind, one that matches our beliefs and goals.

Risk-taking has been stressed as a motivator for personal growth in the pursuit of Nxt. Saying "yes" to scary situations and constantly challenging ourselves to do new things has been identified as a transforming road to become the next version of ourselves.

Furthermore, we've realized that the Nxt journey isn't dependent on the perfect moment. Rather, it is about embracing the moment and taking little, persistent actions toward our goals. We've learnt that it takes personal responsibility, steadfast faith, and perseverance to make our Nxt a reality.

As we conclude this chapter, keep in mind that our Nxt is a never-ending adventure with no end in sight. It is a path of self-realization, self-improvement, and self-discovery. It is the determination to live a life that is true to our actual selves, appreciates our accomplishments, and leaves a meaningful legacy.

So, once you flip the final page of this book, consider it a new beginning rather than an end. Your Nxt adventure continues, and you're better prepared to traverse the route toward your next great thing, your own distinctive Nxt, thanks to the insights and lessons you've gained. It's time to embrace the journey, take the next step, and create a life filled with joy, contentment, and happiness. Your Nxt journey has begun.

Made in United States
Troutdale, OR
09/27/2023

13236084R00040